Passion

Uncover the Potential and Purpose Behind Your Passion.

By Keona A. Henderson

Book Cover by K. Paige

Positive Women Meet Up, LLC

Printed in the United States of America

Published by Positive Women Meet Up, LLC

ISBN: 978-0-578-49237-7

Positive Women Meet Up, LLC
www.PositiveWomenMeetUp.com
Info@PositiveWomenMeetUp.com

Table of Contents

1
Victors, Not Victims

"You are not a victim of your circumstances, you are a product of your decisions." —Keona Henderson

When I was 8 years old, I woke up one day to my mother packing our bags. I could hear her ruffling around in my room while I was sleep. I peeked one eye open and wrapped the covers up around my neck. The sun was just beginning to peak in through my bedroom window, and my mother was in my bedroom, on the floor, haphazardly throwing all of my clothes into a black trash bag with tears running down her face, fidgety hands, and the look of fear in her eyes. My mother is a strong woman. An intelligent woman, a poet. A woman who made a way out of no way. In this moment, she was none of that. She was broken. She was literally, sitting in pieces on my bedroom floor. I immediately knew what was happening. She had finally had enough. She finally decided to leave my father.

My father was a stern man. An intelligent man. Dental hygiene was important to him. Hard in the face. A bushy, black beard covered his jaw. Starched khakis, a white muscle tee, and black house slippers were his daily outfit. The beginning of their relationship was good, I assume. I hear stories of them being madly in love. That was before his erratic behavior and substance abuse. Before he was abusive to my mother, to me, and my siblings.

So here I am laying in my bed and my mother is packing my clothes in a trash bag. It was finally time to go and I knew it. I was not sad. I was happy we would finally be leaving the abuse behind. I got out of bed, grabbed my large framed Kriss Kross poster off the wall and we left. We walked right past my father who laid asleep on the couch, either high or exhausted. Probably high.

Just like that, my mother decided to leave my father, start a new chapter in her life…in our lives. Within hours, we were on a flight to a women's shelter, which became home for my first year as a resident of Texas. My mother may have been ashamed of her circumstances, but she never let that stop her from caring for us, or encouraging us to push through difficulties while pursuing her dreams in the process. Our whole life changed with one decision. That is how quickly your life can change too.

Either for better or worse. You have to make the decision to birth your vision, make your dreams come true, and believe in yourself. My mother always told me and my siblings, "You are not a victim. You are a victor, and you define your future." A victor is a person who defeats an opponent or opposition. As a result of this constant positive affirmation from my mother, I never felt that my past experience with an abusive, drug addicted father, or growing up with a single parent defined me as a person. I didn't dwell on it. This affirmation kept me encouraged. I did not allow others to feel sorry for me and I did not feel sorry for myself. I simply made the decision to show up as my best self in this world every day. I was determined that my past would not stop me from achieving my goals. We all go through things. Albeit, some of us go through more things than others.

Understand this: Every decision in your life has led up to this very moment. Every decision ahead of this moment will be a part of the thread that creates your future.

Use that as fuel to ignite your fire. Use this workbook as inspiration to follow your dreams. Do not allow your past to continue to victimize you in your future. The longer you procrastinate on your goals, the longer you will be living in the shadow of who you are meant to be. Decide to be a victor, instead of a victim.

Victors, Not Victims Questionnaire

1. Who are you? *Describe yourself in detail.*

2. How does who you are relate to your passion?

3. What would it look like for you to show up, every day, as a victor?

Passion2Purpose Workbook:
Uncover the Potential and Purpose Behind Your Passion

4. Name the past successes you are most proud of.

5. What struggles have you gone through on your way to success?

6. What sacrifices have you made in order to succeed?

7. How do you feel after accomplishing your goals?

8. What keeps you from quitting?

9. What are a list of things you would you do if you knew you wouldn't fail?

10. What are you most scared of in regards to pursuing your passion?

11. Write a story about a time in your life that was hard, but you didn't quit.

2
Just Start

"Starting today can mean success tomorrow."
— Keona Henderson

When I started Positive Women Meet Up, there was no LLC attached and I had no idea that I would be where I am now—hosting ticketed events with dynamic speakers and sponsors, a website, renting venues, consulting on projects with clients, an established LLC, and the list goes on. All I knew is that I wanted to encourage women to network with each other. My first "meet up" was at a movie theatre in Rancho Cucamonga, California. I invited my women friends, family, and coworkers for an evening of networking. I posted the invite on social media. I called, text, and sent emails to all of the women I knew and made a flyer from my phone. My plan was to watch a movie, and go to dinner afterwards. I got approximately 20 RSVPs for attendance. I was hype! The day of the event, I even received a telephone call on the way to the theatre. One of the ladies I invited called to tell me she was on her way. I arrived and stood in front of the movie theatre for a while, by myself. Eventually three people showed up. One was my sister, one was my best friend, and the third was a guest my best friend brought with her. I waited. I just knew others were coming. What about the woman who called me and said she was on her way? No one else showed up.

The woman didn't answer her phone when I called to see how far she was. My three "attendees" and I enjoyed the movie and dinner together, but I was devastated. Crushed. What happened to all of those RSVPs? That was a very embarrassing moment for me, but looking back on it, I can honestly say that was the most important "meet up" to date for me personally. Why? Because I started. I acted on my goal. I pursued my passion. I birthed my vision.

Understand this: The world doesn't stop just because you do.

Nor does the world pause. The world constantly moves on. If I had decided not to host that movie meet up, I truly believe I would still be dreaming about empowering others and you would not have this workbook in your hands. What is even more sad to think is that I would have procrastinated longer, while others around me pursued their passions and birthed their visions. You know what is even worse?

Someone executing a project that is within your skillset and they do not do it with half of the vigor or execution you would have done it with. You watch them as they climb the ladder to success, with half the talent you have. All because you were too scared, worried, or lazy to pursue your passion. When you decide to show up every day as your best self is when you will make the best of your days and be rewarded.

Just Start Questionnaire

1. What passion project(s) have you been procrastinating on?

   Explain why you have not yet started.

2. What are some things you have always loved to do? Why?

3. What would "just starting" look like for you today?

4. Does your career path align with your passion project? Why or Why not?

5. What tools, talents, and resources do you currently possess that will help you pursue your passion project?

6. Why do you need to pursue your passion project?

7. What members of your family or friends will support you as you pursue your passion project? List their names and how they can support you.

3
Our Friends Are Not Our Clients

"You will receive the most support from people you know the least."
-Keona Henderson

Here is the hard truth— Our passion is not our friend's responsibility. Do not expect your friends to be your clients, your attendees, your volunteers, or your public relations officers. Our friends are our friends. This is a fine line that I encourage you not to mix or cross. Stay out of your feelings on this one. Yes, our friends should be among our supporters and sometimes even our personal cheer squad, but if they aren't interested in attending your event, or purchasing your product/service, do not hate them for it. They are just not interested. Focus your energy on the people who do need your product or service. Those are the people that will be more receptive to hearing about it, supporting it, or purchasing it. These people are your target market or group of consumers in which your product or service is aimed. In addition to your target market, you should get clear on your niche. A niche is a comfortable or suitable position in life or employment; a product or service that appeals to a small, specialized section of the population. For example, your target market could be newlyweds between the ages of 20 and 30, who earn a median income of $50,000 a year and love to travel. Your niche would be teaching newlyweds how to budget to purchase their first home within a year of marriage, while still enjoying a vacation filled lifestyle.

Yes, I expect my friends to show me support. Support looks different for everyone. Support can be shown through time, talent, or treasure. A person can spend time helping you plan or set up your event. They can also lend a hand by using their talents to help you achieve your goals. An example would be working your event, editing your book, or producing your podcast because that is where their passion or area of expertise lies. Lastly, people can show support through treasure, such as a monetary donation or sponsorship, purchasing a product or service from your new business or passion project, or by providing something else of value that will help you achieve your goal.

A long time ago, I believed that support meant my friends should attend every event I hosted, pass out flyers, and post my events on their social media pages. I no longer think that. I realized that when I was working in retail, I did not expect my friends to only shop at my store. When I served as a life coach for people with mental disabilities, I did not expect my friends to also become life coaches. Following your passion and starting your own business is lonely. There will be days and nights when all of your energy goes to making your goals a reality and you will be content. Yet, your friends won't have that same energy about your goals because they do not share your passion. This does not mean your passion project isn't interesting, worthy or profitable. It simply means your friends are not your clients.

Understand this: Your passion will not succeed if you only share it with your friends.

Your purpose is greater than you. Reach out to the world. Do not hide behind your inner circle. Reach out and network within different circles. There is someone in the world who will connect with your story because it's a part of their life too. There is someone in the world who needs the product or service you are going to create. Those are the clients you should locate.

Our Friends Are Not Our Clients Questionnaire

1. What are you passionate about? Why?

2. We need to recognize support when it comes along. What are the types of talents and treasures others can provide to help support your passion project?

3. Who is your target market? Why did you choose this market?

4. How will you target this market?

5. Who is your niche market? Why did you choose this niche?

6. How will you dig into your niche?

7. Why is your passion project important to your target market and niche?

4
Think Differently

"Do the best you can until you know better. Then when you know better, do better." —Maya Angelou

In the early 2000s while in college, I birthed the idea of Positive Women Meet Up. I did not act on it until years later. Why? I shared my new born vision with people before I had my plan together. I was told that a networking event for women was not a good idea, that it would be impossible to get women together to empower one another, collaborate, and support one another. I focused on what others thought of my idea and became discouraged. As a result, I slept on my idea and tucked it away. I continued to dream about it, think about it, and consider how many opportunities I had passed up for approximately 8 years.

Often, we have an idea that comes to us randomly and clearly. The first thought of the idea is in its purest form and we get excited about it. Then we divulge our idea, in all of its greatness, to the public without fully investing ourselves in our vision. We have a wide smile on our face and we're waiting for others to see the vision and give us approval or encouragement. What really happens is after we share our vision, the person starts to ask questions we never thought of and all of a sudden, our great idea, in its purest form, seems so complicated and not such a good idea anymore. Then we give in to self-limiting beliefs by picking apart our vision before we give it a chance to thrive.

STOP THAT!

No one achieves their goals by listening to all of the criticism around them. You have to imagine yourself in better circumstances. Imagine yourself successful. Imagine how you will feel after achieving your goals. Focus on preparing your vision, researching the tools needed to birth your vision, and executing your vision.

Understand this:
In pursuit of your passion, you must think differently, prepare differently, and research differently in order to execute differently.

Protect that vision like a newborn baby until you are ready to act on it. Imagine you just birthed a baby. Are you going to introduce your baby to every person you meet and ask them to approve of your baby? Are you going to ask people to critique your baby and give you feedback about your baby? No. You want to protect the baby for as long as you can. I want you to protect your new born idea in the same way. Protect your idea until you have a solid plan for it and the idea is in action. Protect it until it's developed enough to stand up on its own. This means you have to work hard. You can't think about the vision for a year. Act on it immediately, create an action plan and develop it as you go. Have faith in your plan.

What is your plan?

You will develop your plan by getting clear on your vision and thinking differently. You will develop your plan by preparing, researching, and executing a vital part of your routine. If you constantly think you are going to fail, you will. Those negative words you think or speak to yourself will enter your spirit and grow into an emotional block. If you constantly concern yourself with who is supportive of your passion project and who is not, you will fail. If you concern yourself with those who failed to support your vision, you will lose focus of your goal. If you are pursuing this passion project wishing to impress others or receive attention, you are subject to failure. The road to your goals is long and rocky with unexpected twists and turns. You may start to doubt yourself and your vision. You may begin to think of all the reasons it won't work. You may procrastinate. You may become confused. Stay the course and continue to think differently. Fight the urge to give in to self-limiting beliefs.

Let go of the expectations others have for you. If you have a vision you are passionate about, you must pursue it. People will never know you are a graphic designer, artist, writer, singer, actor, motivational speaker, poet, designer, or creative until you open your mouth and say it— LOUDLY.

Think Differently Questionnaire

1. What expectations do you have for yourself?

2. What is your passion?

3. What expectations do you have for your passion project or business?

4. Are you currently pursuing your passion? How so?

5. In the past, have you let others discourage you from pursuing your passion? *Explain how and why.*

6. What is your passion project or business idea? *Explain in great detail.*

7. What excites you about this passion project or business idea? Why is your idea excellent?

8. What are the foreseeable weak points in your business plan? How could you potentially fail?

9. Why will you succeed with this passion project or business?

10. Who is your competition and why?

11. What is your detailed action plan? What date will you start putting your plan into action?

5
Qualify Yourself

"You don't need anyone's permission, besides your own, to pursue your passion." —Keona Henderson

We have been brainwashed to think we are not good enough. Not because of facts, but because of fear. Fear of the unknown. Fear of failure. Fear of success. What if you knew you couldn't fail? Would that jumpstart you? The jumpstart for me to qualify myself came when a close family member said "Why don't you think people will come to your event? You have the skills for this. Just start."

That night I listed all my personal qualifications and experiences. I pumped myself up and I created what I call my "passion" resume. I did this and YOU can too! You do not need permission to be great.

Understand this: You are the only person qualified enough to bring your passion to purpose.

We all have professional resumes that we use to convince companies to hire us, pay us, and give us benefits. A resume is something everyone should have; however, I encourage you to create your *passion* resume in addition to your professional resume. Most of us were taught how to work in order to support someone else's dream, either through a job, school, church, or within our family. Rarely are we taught to qualify ourselves and follow our own dreams to be successful. A *"passion resume"* helps you qualify yourself.

My passion resume includes all of my personal qualifications. It is difficult thing to chisel all of your experience, talent, education, and accomplishments down to one or two pages for a professional resume. My passion resume does not have a page limit, and it showcases the things I find a natural interest in -- my talents, hobbies, and passions. The first step is knowing you are what you say you are. How do you know you are what you say you are? List your qualifications. What do you have experience in? This is not a chance for you to make things up. You wouldn't go around telling people you're a lawyer and you haven't passed the bar exam. Don't embarrass yourself. Be honest with yourself about your skills and talents. This is a chance to highlight the things you hold the creative advantage or extensive experience in.

For example, I am qualified in public speaking. I've spoken at many events since the age of nine. When I was 16 years old, I won 1st place at the Vocational Industrial Clubs of America (VICA) speech competition for the State of Tennessee. I went on to college, where I excelled in public speaking classes. I polished my craft by performing my poetry in front of live audiences. Since college, I have hosted events, served on panels, and served as keynote speaker many times over. I now host my own women empowerment events and develop aspiring speakers. I am a qualified public speaker.

I am now giving you permission to qualify yourself. Did your grandmother teach you how to sew at age 8 and you've polished that craft over the years? Do you alter and sew clothes for a living or as your side hustle? You're a seamstress, my dear. As a child, you often made up dance routines in your living room with your friends, and later took a few dance classes. You now have a YouTube channel where you feature your original choreographed routines. You're a choreographer, my dear.

Employers did not care about my passion for women empowerment. They certainly did not care that I wrote and performed poetry. Neither did they care that I won first place in a high school state speech competition, but I care and I'm following my passion. When I completed my passion resume and realized that I had the experience to qualify myself to pursue my passions, the fire inside of me was burning so bright. I couldn't do anything without thinking about embarking on my passion project.

Understand this: Making up rules as to why you are not qualified to pursue your passion is self-sabotage.

Do not allow self-limiting beliefs to hold you back before you even start. There is no instruction manual when pursuing your passion. There is no blueprint. If there was a blueprint to success, everyone would be following their passions. Instead, only a select few take the leap of faith to follow their passion. The majority will be left to wonder what greatness they could have embarked upon if they would have followed their dreams.

We have all followed different paths and few can tell you exactly what steps they took that led them to success. Everyone's path is riddled with dead ends, poor decisions, confusion, low self-esteem, hurdles, successes, expenses, and many failed attempts.

I know a fashion stylist who worked at Forever 21, he was eventually fired, but later got his shot as a celebrity stylist after several years of struggling. Another fashion stylist who went to FDIM, earned a degree, and went on to become a celebrity stylist. That opportunity snowballed into more celebrity gigs. Another stylist worked hard for 10 years learning to sew, selling their own designs, and doing odd jobs such as modeling, dancing, acting, and washing dishes. Eventually she was hired on a hit reality television show. That opportunity changed her life in under a year and she now has the eyes of the world on her. Everyone has a different journey.

Lastly, thoughts become things. If you think you're going to succeed you will. If you think you're going to fail, you will. You must give yourself permission to qualify yourself. I have created a permission slip for you. Anytime you feel inadequate or allow self-limiting beliefs to sink in, take a look at your permission slip.

I, _____, give
myself permission to follow my dreams.
My passion is

_____

_____

_____.

I am committed to walking in my
passion. I will work hard until I succeed.
I have permission to follow my dreams.

X_____

Sign and date

Qualify Yourself Questionnaire

1. What are some reasons people fail to pursue their passion?

2. Why are you pursuing your passion?

3. Why is your passion important to you? Why is it important to others?

4. What steps do you feel will lead you to success while walking in your purpose?

5. How have you practiced self-sabotaging behaviors in the past?
   List those self-sabotaging behaviors.

6. How will you avoid self-sabotaging behaviors in the future and walk in your purpose?

7. Create several positive affirmations directly related to succeeding within your passion.

Example: Every time I, try I succeed.
     "No" means "Next opportunity."

8. Create a personal resume proving you're qualified to pursue your business idea or passion project.

Objective (Your passion):
Identify your passion and explain, in detail, how you will use that passion to birth your vision.

Experience:
List all of the opportunities you have been provided, which allow you to walk in your purpose.
(IE: Speaking engagements, publishing a book, hosting events, booking clients, etc.)

Education:
List any formal or informal training you have received that will aid you as you follow your purpose.

Honors/Awards/Certificates:
List any awards, and certificates you have received that align with your passion.

References: List positive family, friends, co-workers, peers and mentors in your life who have witnessed you walking in your purpose, and can provide a positive review of your skills.

Personal Resume

Personal Resume

Personal Resume

6
Leverage Your Resources

"Networking is about connecting, not collecting."
-Keona Henderson

Birthing your vision is like birthing your first child — scary and painful. Starting on your passion project can be scary, and at times people choose to go at it alone. Have you ever heard the term "go half on a baby"? Well apply that same resourcefulness to pursuing your passion. It may be less fun than baby making, but it will give your dream what it needs to thrive and survive.

Many of us have the vision, but lack funds to make anything happen. Exercise your right to leverage your resources. Your resources are your network-friends, family members, and associates. For example, if you want to write a book and have a friend who is a great writer, ask them to edit your book. There may be a fee, but it would be considerably cheaper than if you hire a firm. If that's what it takes to export the information from your brain to a book, do it. If you have an associate who has a great testimony or solid expertise in a subject you need for your business, partner with them and trade work for work. Alternatively, there may be organizations in your community that offer free or inexpensive resources. We all have resources at our disposal that we under-utilize or fail to utilize.

In 2015, I decided to revamp Positive Women Meet Up. I changed it from the literal "meet up" to a ticketed event with speakers and sponsors. My goal was to provide women a platform to pursue their passion and be recognized for it. I leveraged my resources by utilizing free and inexpensive books for research. I began visiting bookstores to research marketing, branding, and professional development. I knew what I knew, but what I didn't know, I had to learn. I've always loved attending women empowerment events. I attended more women empowerment events and reflected critically on the event upon departure. I thought about what could've made the event better for me as an attendee. In this case, I leveraged my resources by surveying "the competition." I knew dynamic women in my area who were pursuing their passion, walking in their purpose, and had a passion that deserved a platform. I contacted those dynamic women and offered them a platform for empowerment. I leveraged my resources by creating a platform to showcase powerful women while empowering them in the process. Those dynamic women told other dynamic women and my event and brand became increasingly popular.

Understand this: In addition to qualifying yourself, you can also qualify those around you. If you value their talent or expertise, show them.

You should be constantly talking about your passion. When you are asked what you do, talk about your passion. Whenever appropriate, insert your passion into a conversation. Ask others what they do, then open up an opportunity to talk about what you do. Change your signature in your phone or email. Get new business cards with your passion title on it and hand them to everyone you meet. You must put yourself in the position you want to be in. Again, qualify yourself. The more people hear you talk about your passion and the more you position yourself to work within your passion, the quicker you will be known for your passion. If you are looking for a resource, tell everyone you meet what that resource is. They may know someone who can provide it. If nothing else, you are getting the word out about your passion and what you do. You are a walking billboard. Free advertisement, use it!

Leverage Your Resources Questionnaire

1. Are you an expert in your field of passion? Why or why not? If you're not, what can you do to become an expert?

2. What free resources can you leverage to assist you with your passion project?

3. What low cost or inexpensive resources can you leverage to assist you with your passion project?

4. Do you currently have the manual resources to pursue your passion project?

5. What resources do you need in order for your passion project to succeed?

6. What books have you read about pursuing your passion project? How have they helped you? List some books you should read.

7. What do you need in a mentor?
   Describe your perfect mentor.

8. Who do you have in your network, who are experts in your field of passion? How can you learn from them or connect with them?

9. What tradeshows, workshops or conferences deal directly with your passion?
List their respective locations, and event dates. Plan to attend.

10. Do you talk about your passion to everyone you meet? If you do, what do you tell them? If not, what would you tell them?

7
Stay in Your Lane

"I know what I know and what I don't know, I don't pretend to know."
-Keona Henderson

I have always been honest about knowing what I know and what I do not know. I do not pretend to know anything. I am curious about everything. In 2013, my only goal was to unify women. Along the way, my vision evolved. I worked on maintaining the focus of my vision and allowing that to lead me in all my decisions for Positive Women Meet Up. For anything else I envisioned for Positive Women Meet Up, and did not know, I researched or consulted with a mentor. I became clear on my vision. I decided what Positive Women Meet Up looked like as an event, what I wanted it to feel like for the attendees, how I wanted attendees to feel when they left, and what kind of speakers my audience needed.

One element that distracted me early on was comparing my goals for PWM to someone else's accomplishments within their own passion project. I felt like other people were gaining more traction than I, had more supporters than I, and had more experience. I warn you—If you get caught up in another person's path, you will encounter unfamiliar territory that you are not prepared for. You will get distracted. You will no longer be in your lane.

Understand this: It may appear that another person is excelling rapidly. This is from the outside looking in. Their goals are not your goals and their decisions are not your decisions.

As drivers, we should keep our eyes on the road ahead of us at all times. We should be aware of cautions that may arise such as road blocks, lane changes, our next exit, and our final destination. We have all been there-- The lane next to us seems to be moving faster so we switch lanes and then everything in that new lane slows down, almost suddenly with our arrival. Stay in your lane. No matter what your goal is, if you believe in it wholeheartedly and believe you can achieve it, go for it. Do not be easily distracted or disappointed because of the achievements others may garner or the opportunities that seem to fall in their lap. Be happy in your space and progress will come. Your focus will affect every decision you make and every opportunity you receive. If you stay in focused in your lane, you are bound to arrive at your destination.

Stay in Your Lane Questionnaire

1. What is your vision for your passion project in 5 years? 10 years?

2. When do you feel triggered to compare yourself to others?
Explain when and why.

3. What education, skills, talents, resources, and knowledge do you possess to help you achieve your goals?

4. What are three action items that will help you focus on your goals consistently?

5. What are your top three goals – short-term, mid-term and long term?

6. Develop a timeline to achieve these goals.

List your start dates, and end dates for your short-term, mid-term and long-term goals. Also, provide a date at the half way mark to check for progress and re-evaluate.

7. How will you reward yourself when you accomplish your goals?
List the reward for your short-term, mid-term and long-term goals.

8. Describe the feeling you will have when you accomplish each goal.

8
Protect Your Peace

"Once you stop treating yourself as average, you will step into excellence."
-Keona Henderson

You are reading this right now because you are not average. You want more out of your life. You have goals, you are a creative and you want to enjoy a life you do not need to take a break from. This is a brave thing you're doing. Creating from scratch. Following your dreams. Pursuing your goals. Walking in your purpose. Birthing your vision. It is something most people aren't comfortable doing because it requires one to become uncomfortable. The space you create to pursue your passion is just big enough to allow self-limiting beliefs to creep in. Do not allow this to happen. Protect your peace, follow your passion and walk in your purpose.

Your passion is the one thing you can't stop thinking about. You dream about it and it follows you everywhere. No matter where you go, you find yourself operating in your passion. While writing this, I'm approaching my ninth year as a sworn Probation Officer, I often find myself empowering the youth I come in contact with. Most think of law, arrests, or court when they hear "Probation Officer." Empowerment is very likely not a word that comes to mind. Yet, empowerment is my purpose. No matter what I'm doing or who I'm talking to, empowerment pours out of me. In order to walk in my purpose and have empowerment to pour, I must protect my peace. I can't do anything for anyone if I'm not at peace and in line with my passion.

Following your passion is difficult enough with your own self-doubt and uncertainty. Adding the opinions of others will only make it worse. Considering the opinion of others regarding your passion project, will allow doubt to creep in, which will cause you to hesitate and lose faith in your vision. Once you make the leap from employee to CEO, follower to leader, or dreamer to doer, your environment will change. Some people will not understand your passion and will say negative or discouraging things to you. Some people will envy the courage you exhibited by choosing to follow your passion, and will attempt to discourage you because they are too scared to follow their own passions. There will be people who will be nasty, negative naysayers. They will drain you with *their* self-limiting beliefs and suck the energy out of you with their issues, neediness and instability. These types of people usually lack self-confidence, are unsure of their own passions and goals, and look for happiness in others instead of within themselves. If they aren't doing anything, they don't want you to do anything. If they don't know what their passion is, they will be upset that you have found out what yours is. They will make you feel like following your passion is the wrong choice. Take steps to stay away from people, places, and things that cause your peace to be disrupted. Following your heart is about protecting your peace of mind. Do you want to wonder "What if?" all your life? Do you want to operate in someone else's vision of you? Do you only want to experience your wildest dreams, while dreaming? Or do you want to live your dream in real life? Do you want to do what you are passionate about every day? To walk in your purpose, you must first follow your passion. To follow your passion, you must **protect your peace.**

While protecting your peace, be nice to yourself. You will encounter people who seem to have their stuff together. They are also fighting through the transitions instead of giving up or procrastinating. That is the space that dreams come true in. When you choose every day to follow your passion, despite the hardships you may endure, you're on the right path. That's when you know you are walking in your purpose. Your passion should be something that you do because it feels good, not because it pays you.

You will encounter people who see that you are focused on your passion and may be inspired by your determination. You can't help anyone else if you don't know your passion and haven't aligned with your purpose. Helping someone find their passion or live out their dream will become draining for you and you may even start to resent helping them. When I am struggling to protect my peace, my favorite cousin often reminds me that on every flight, the flight attendant instructs every passenger to put their own oxygen mask on first before helping others in an emergency. That is true in life and business as well. Protect your peace. Make sure you are stable before helping someone else pursue their goals.

Protect Your Peace Questionnaire

1. List the type of qualities the people in your inner circle should have:

2. Have you identified the nasty, negative naysayers in your circle? What negative qualities do they have? (Recognize these personality traits in the future and steer clear of them).

3. How has their negative attitude affected you thus far?

4. When are you going to leave these people behind? How will you sever those ties in order to protect your peace?

5. Why is it important to dissociate yourself from such people?

6. What type of people will enhance you and support your goals?
   Describe the type of person in depth.

7. Why would this type of person benefit you and your goals?

8. Where can you find the type of person that will benefit you and your goals?

9. Who do you know that already fits this description?
    Identify them by name and explain their positive qualities.

10. How will you protect your peace?

List actionable steps you can take to protect your peace from people, places, or things that may cause your peace to be disrupted.

9
Give Yourself Permission

"Let go of fear and face the facts."- Keona Henderson

I've spoken to many women with great ideas that didn't believe in themselves enough to follow through. Some women never move in the direction of their passions. They never establish their goal as a tangible task because they're scared or waiting for someone else to co-sign their passion project.

Understand this: You only need permission from yourself to be great.

When I decided to revamp Positive Women Meet Up, I doubted myself. After two years of dinner with the girls, or an informal movie meet up, I transformed it to an actual event, with reserved seats, tickets, and themed topics. I was often plagued with self-limiting beliefs, such as thoughts of how other people may have been more qualified than me to produce this event. Who was going to buy a ticket to my event? Where would I find attendees? Were women even interested? I had a hard time getting women to come to a movie for free. How was I going to convince women to purchase a ticket to my event? I settled on throwing away my doubts and I began to qualify myself.

As a child, we look up to our parents for our first nuggets of approval. When we get older, we attend school, where we wait on our teachers and professors to grade our papers. We wait for them to approve our thought processes, ideas and writing styles. Not only approve, but to assign a value to it as well. That value tells us how well we did. We take that value and use it to determine how smart we are in comparison to our peers. Life keeps going and eventually, we get a job where we receive quarterly or annual evaluations, again to approve our thought processes, ideas and writing styles, and to assign a value to our work. We take that value and use it to determine how smart we are in comparison to our peers.

We are taught to be workers and to constantly seek approval. We are taught our work is not good unless someone tells us it is good. We are taught that if our work does not mirror that of our peers, it must be wrong. Your passion project is not wrong. Your creative ideas are not wrong. Your passion and creativity is the one thing you have full control over approving and assigning value to. Whether personally or professionally, we should always strive to continue learning, improving and putting our best effort forward. Give yourself permission to be great! When it comes to your passions, you never need to wait for approval or understanding from others. Do not wait for someone to tell you "Good job." Qualify yourself.

Give Yourself Permission
Questionnaire

1. How are you qualified to pursue your passion? *List your education, talents, skills, etc.*

2. Do you want to be great? *Explain why.*

3. Have you given yourself permission to be great? What actionable steps can you take to give yourself permission to be great?
Start on my passion project, host my first event, write and publish my book, create your first prototype, etc.

4. Who is in charge of approving your thought processes, ideas and assigning value to your work? Why?

5. Do you believe in yourself? What steps have you taken or can you take to show that you believe in yourself?

6. Why do you believe in yourself?

10
Exit Your Comfort Zone

"Don't die holding onto your gift. Present it to the world."
-Keona Henderson

To be excellent you have to do things you've never done before, and do things that many people won't do. To be successful you have to get uncomfortable.

In 2015, my vision for Positive Women Meet Up became crystal clear. I knew I wanted to empower more women and provide a platform for empowerment. To do this, I also had to leave my comfort zone. At the time, my comfort zone was hosting an informal meetup with low attendance. The informal meet up didn't call for me to make a substantial investment, nor did it call for me to invest a substantial amount of time to make it happen. As a result, I wasn't meeting new women, and I wasn't empowering women. I had to level up. I had to invest in my goal if I wanted it to grow. That's when I decided to transform my informal meet up into a full event. It was scary.

I had experience planning events, and I was comfortable speaking in front of large groups. I went with what I knew. I considered past women empowerment events I attended, what I felt like they were missing, and how I felt as an attendee. I created an event that I would want to attend. Next, I obtained a domain name for the website, designed the site myself, secured an event space and sold tickets to cover costs. Many people doubted the leap of faith I took. At times, I did too. I began to budget wiser in order to save for event expenses from my paychecks. I had to overcome the uncomfortable feeling in order to achieve my goals. I had to ignore the negative comments and unsolicited suggestions from people who thought selling tickets to this event was a bad idea. Admittedly, I wasn't totally sure myself, but I knew I wanted PWM to be better and different. My vision was clear. For the first two years I did what I was comfortable with and what I felt worked at the time. After many failed attempts, small turnouts, and wasted money, I took it up a notch and bet on myself. I knew I could do better. Making those changes allowed me to learn more about event production, and within a year of the first change, I made a few more changes. I did not wait for someone to tell me changes were needed. I created the change I wanted to see.

Understand this: Exit your comfort zone. Nothing is happening there.

What is your comfort zone? Are you always behind on work because you spend hours scrolling through social media every day? Do you miss opportunities to achieve your goals because of poor time management? Do you refer others for a project you were too scared to take on? Do you spend time socializing instead of polishing your craft? Do you budget before spending or spend without caution? Do you complain about your lack of funds, progress, support and success without making appropriate adjustments? Do you seek mentorship, and further education that will equip you with the necessary tools to level up? Do you network with like-minded individuals? Within the answers to these questions lies your comfort zone.

Exit Your Comfort Zone
Questionnaire

1. Explain your comfort zone. *Be honest with yourself.*

2. Why do you need to do **TODAY** in order to exit your comfort zone?

3. What are you willing to sacrifice in order to exit your comfort zone? *Explain.*

4. Are you comfortable with doing new things in the pursuit of your goals? Why or why not?

5. What are some of the things, in pursuit of your goals, that you will have to do, but have never done before?

6. Why should you value doing new things or uncomfortable things on your journey to success?

7. Have you been doing your absolute best at pursuing your goals? How so?

11
Goal Planning

"There will always be something else to achieve. Focus on one step at a time."
-Keona Henderson

You should have many goals. Your goals should range from the short-term goals (hourly, daily, weekly, monthly) to the long-term goals (1 year, 5 years, 10 years). The short-term goals should all be smaller steps to achieve the long-term goal.

Understand this: Focus on one goal at a time.

Goal planning is a powerful tool to help you map out and achieve your goals. Goal planning equips you with short-term motivation for your long-term goals. Planning allows you to decide precisely what you want to achieve, what steps you need to take, how you will work to achieve them and where you should concentrate your efforts. Additionally, goal planning will highlight the problem areas and distractions. To begin goal planning, keep in mind that goals should always be **S.M.A.R.T.** : **Specific. Measurable. Achievable. Relevant. Time-bound.**

Specific: Be detailed when identifying your goals.

Measurable: Identify how you will know if you have successfully achieved each goal.

Achievable: Create goals that are realistic, both in regards to the development and deadlines.

Relevant: Be sure that your goals are directly connected to your long-term goal.

Time-bound: Specify how much time it should take you to complete each short-term goal and long-term goal by assigning a deadline.

First, you must define your "big picture" by setting your long-term goal(s). In example, *"Become a world renowned motivational speaker who travels internationally for six months each year empowering women."* Be specific. Next, you'll determine the smaller goals, working in reverse by the year, month, week, and day, listing items that need to be completed in order to make your major goals come to fruition. Your success will be found in the small goals you commit to completing in your daily, weekly, monthly and yearly routine. Over time, each small goal you achieve will add up to the ultimate achievement of the larger goal. With major focus, positive thinking and determination, you will achieve success.

Goal Planning Questionnaire

1. What is your long-term goal?
   Be specific and explain your big picture.

2. List the smaller goals you want to achieve annually to lead you to
    your long-term goal.
    List their deadlines.

3. What daily activities should you do, that when compounded, will produce your ultimate goal?
   IE: Save $X money, take X classes, produce content X times a week/month, etc.

4. What roadblocks, trials or tribulations may interfere with you completing your goals?
   (IE: Procrastination, lack of funds, etc.)

5. How can you prepare now in order to prevent or avoid those roadblocks, trials and tribulations?

Passion2Purpose Affirmations

Reflect on these positive affirmations in times of self-doubt, self-sabotage, and distraction.

I approve of myself.

I am becoming a better me every day.

I am beautiful. I am valuable. I am talented. I am worthy of respect.

I continue to get better and better at everything I do.

If I try, I will succeed.

I succeed at everything I try.

The tools I need to succeed are in my possession.

There is nobody better to get the job done than me.

My strength is bigger than any struggle.

I was not made to give up. I am fearless.

I inspire others.

I don't fear the fire, I am the fire.

I choose what I become. I have the power to change my story.

I use my failures as stepping stones.

I will stop apologizing for being myself.

I do not bow down to my fears.

It is not their job to like me, it is mine.

I am not my mistakes.

I choose to be happy and completely love myself today.

NOTES

NOTES

Made in the USA
Middletown, DE
07 June 2022